WHO AM I?

Who am I?

Titles in the series

Black-and-White (Panda)
Furry and Fluffy-tailed (Rabbit)
Long-necked and Lean (Giraffe)
Winged and Wild (Golden Eagle)

I am long-necked and lean, tall as a tree.
I live in Africa.

WHO AM I?

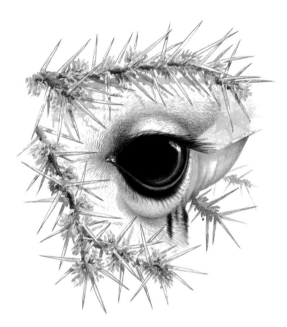

By Moira Butterfield
Illustrated by Wayne Ford

Thameside Press

Distributed in the United States by
Smart Apple Media
1980 Lookout Drive
North Mankato, MN 56003

ISBN 1-930643-92-6

Library of Congress Control Number 2002 141346

Printed by South China Printing Co. Ltd., Hong Kong

Editor: Stephanie Bellwood
Designer: Helen James
Illustrator: Wayne Ford / Wildlife Art Agency
Consultant: Steve Pollock

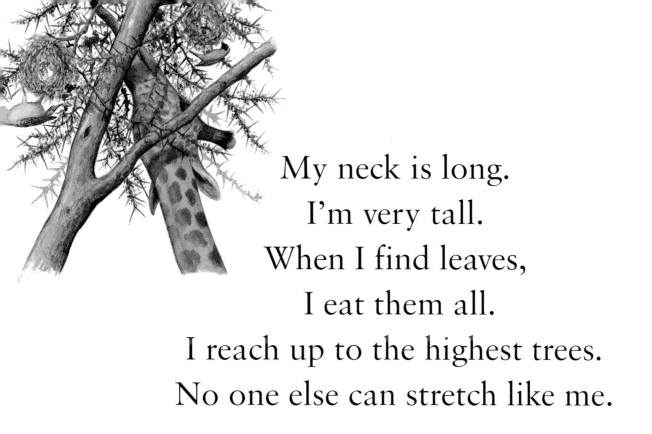

My neck is long.
I'm very tall.
When I find leaves,
I eat them all.
I reach up to the highest trees.
No one else can stretch like me.

Who am I?

Here is my neck.

It is very, very long.
I am the tallest
animal in the world.
I am more than twice
as tall as a man.

I can stretch
to the treetops.
There are lots
of tasty leaves
there that no one
else can reach.

7

Here is my tongue.

Look how long it is.
I curl it round a tree
branch and pull the
leaves into my mouth.

I grind up the leaves
with my teeth. Then
I spend a long time
chewing them.

9

Here is my skin.

I am covered with brown patches called markings. They make me very hard to see among the trees.

A little oxpecker bird sometimes sits on my shoulder. It gobbles up the insects that land on my skin.

Here is my eye.

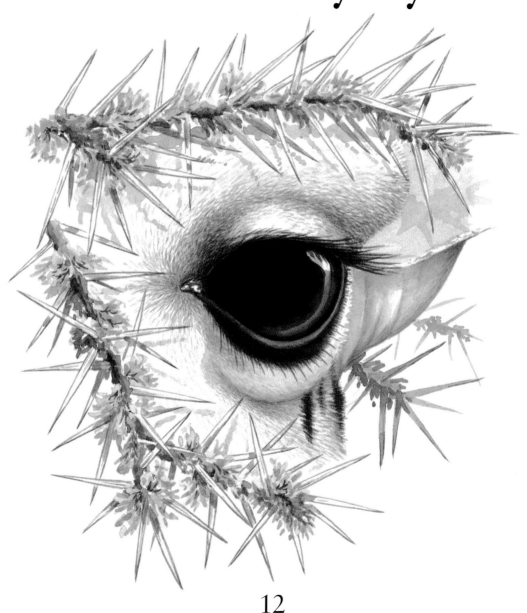

I look out for
hungry lions who
might attack me.
Can you see one
hiding in the grass?

I often close my eyes and
have a short nap. I can't
sleep for long in case
a lion catches me.

Here are my legs.

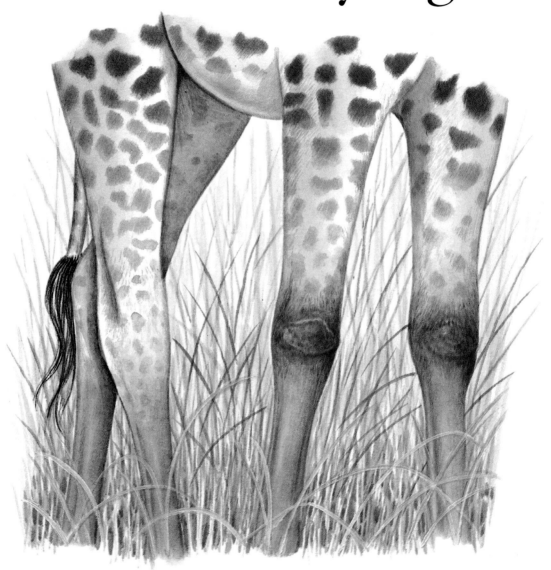

They are thin and
long. When I run
I take giant strides.
I gallop faster than
a lion can run.

I have to spread
my front legs wide
apart when I put
my head down for
a drink of water.

15

Here is my hoof.

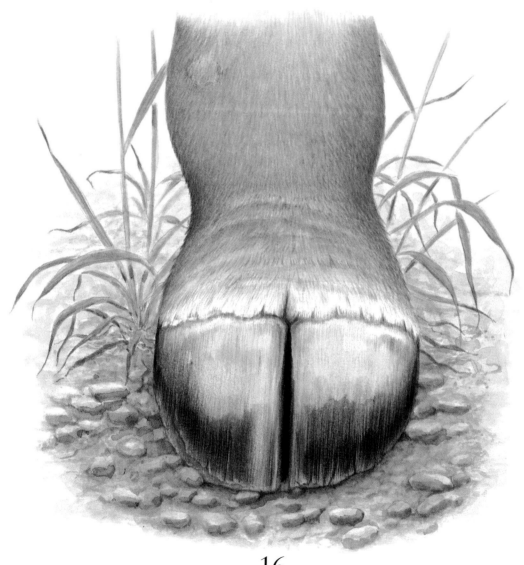

My hoofs are very hard. When my enemies attack me, I give them painful kicks with my hoofs.

If I see one of my enemies, I gallop away. My tough hoofs help me to run a long way.

17

Here is my tail.

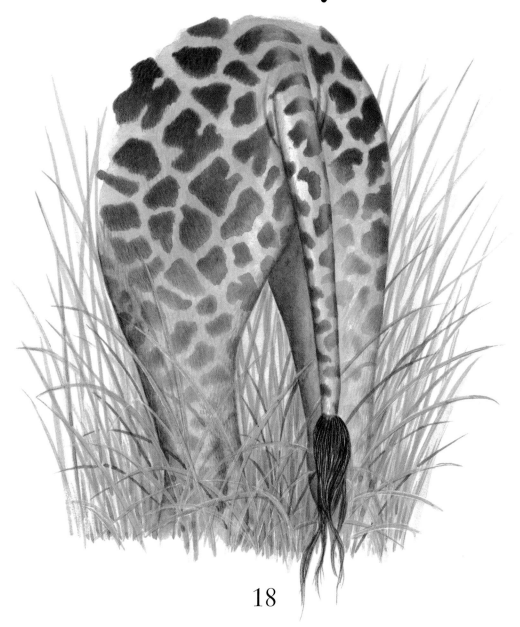

When I feel frightened, I swish my tail and curl it up behind me.

I stretch my long legs and...

gallop away!

Have you guessed who I am?

I am a giraffe.

Point to my…

swishing tail

thick hoofs

large eyes

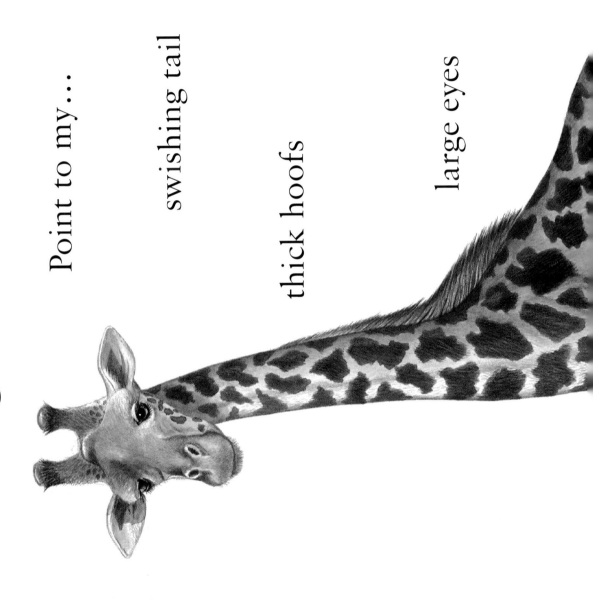

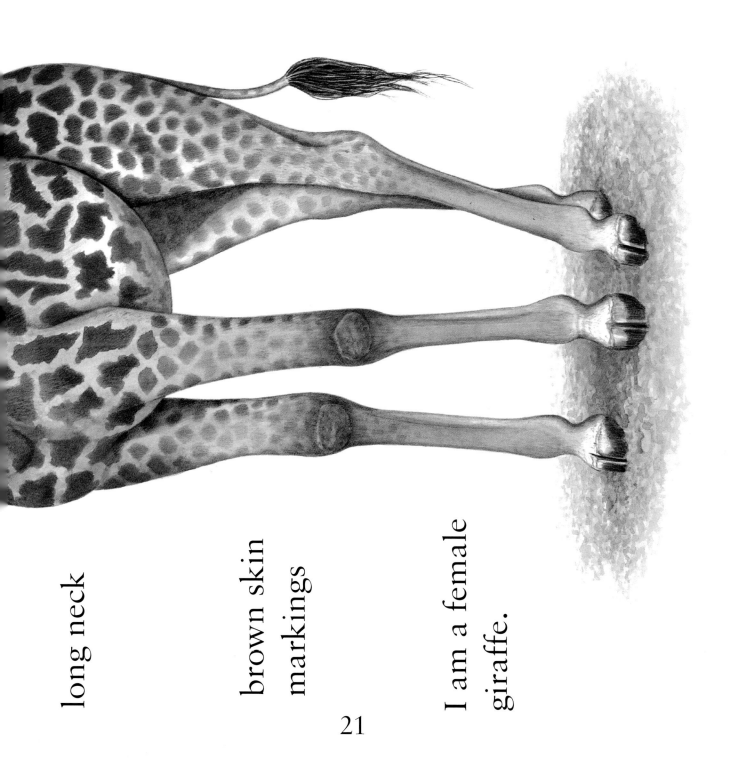

long neck

brown skin
markings

I am a female
giraffe.

21

Here is my baby.

She is called a calf.
She stays with me
and drinks my milk
until she has grown
tall and strong.

Lions and leopards
would like to catch
my calf. I look
after her carefully.

Here is my home.
I live on a grassy plain.

How many giraffes can you see?
Look for two zebras, two baby lions,
and six animals with horns called
Thompson's gazelles.

Here is a map of the world.

I live in a part
of Africa.
Where is my
home on the map?

Can you point to the
place where you live?

Africa

27

Can you answer these questions about me?

What do I like to eat?

Who are my enemies?

How do I stop
my enemies
attacking me?

How many hoofs
do I have?

Where do I live?

What is my
baby called?

What is the name of the little
bird who sometimes sits
on my shoulder?

What does the
little bird do?

Here are some words to learn about me.

attack To try and kill something. Some animals attack other animals and eat them.

calf The name for a baby giraffe.

female An animal that can give birth to babies. Girls and women are female. Boys and men are male.

grind To crush something into small pieces. Giraffes grind leaves with their strong teeth.

gallop To run fast. Animals with hoofs often gallop.

hoof The thick, hard layer that some animals have on the bottom of each foot.

markings The shapes and colors an animal has on its skin. A giraffe has brown markings that look like patches.

plain Land that is wide, flat, and grassy.

stretch To reach out for something. Giraffes stretch to reach for leaves.

INDEX